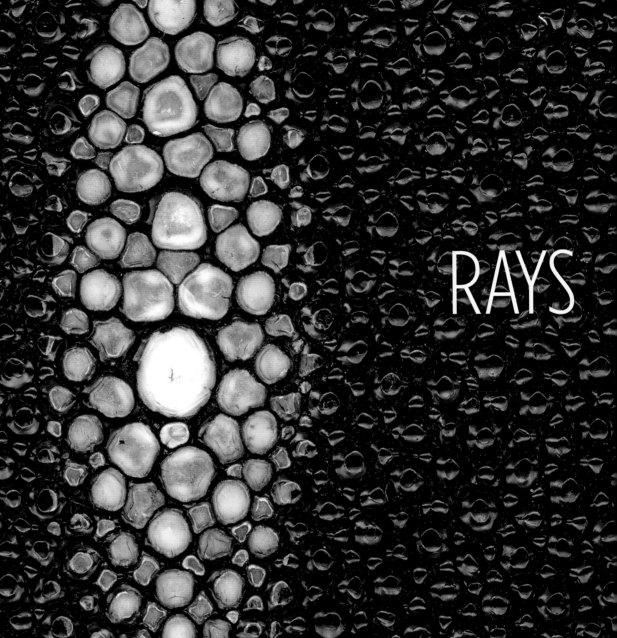

RAYS

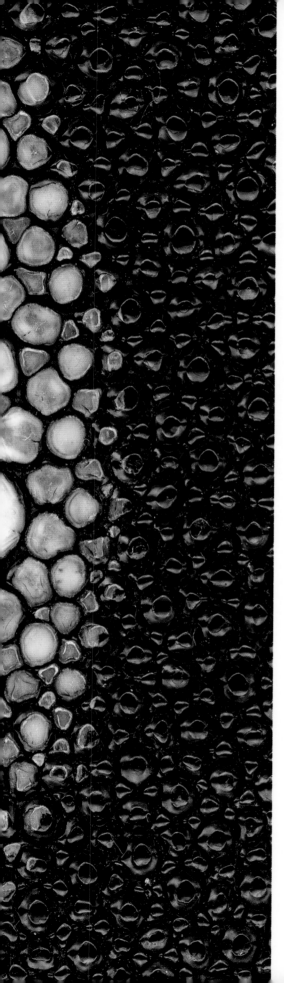

LIVING WILD

Published by Creative Education and Creative Paperbacks
P.O. Box 227, Mankato, Minnesota 56002
Creative Education and Creative Paperbacks are imprints of The Creative Company
www.thecreativecompany.us

Design and production by Mary Herrmann
Art direction by Rita Marshall
Printed in China

Photographs by Alamy (Todd Winner), Creative Commons Wikimedia (AlfvanBeem, Franklin Samir Dattein, Diliff, David Finch, Johnmartindavies, Jstuby, Karelj, Utagawa Kuniyoshi, Ophelia2, Steve Ryan, toadlady1, U.S. Fish and Wildlife Service Headquarters, Ono Yuta), FishBase (Hamid Badar Osmany), Getty Images (Visuals Unlimited, Inc./Louise Murray), iStockphoto (AlexanderZam, crisod, EdStock, JudiLen, Mark Kostich, Nicki1982, sframephoto, Predrag Vuckovic, Wolfgang_Steiner), Navsource (Bureau of Ships Collections/ U.S. National Archives), NOAA (SEFSC Pascagoula Laboratory/Collection of Brandi Noble/ NOAA/NMFS/SEFSC), Shutterstock (Adwo, Brandelet, Ethan Daniels, Durden Images, eyeretina, Leonardo Gonzalez, haveseen, Jung Hsuan, jim808080, J'nel, stephan kerkhofs, LauraD, Louis W, NataLT, Amanda Nicholls, serg_dibrova, totophotos, Edwin van Wier)

Library of Congress Cataloging-in-Publication Data
Gish, Melissa.
Rays / Melissa Gish.
p. cm. — (Living wild)
Includes bibliographical references and index.
Summary: A look at rays, including their habitats, physical characteristics such as their flat, flexible skeletons, behaviors, relationships with humans, and their wide range of hunting tactics in the world today.

ISBN 978-1-60818-708-9 (hardcover)
ISBN 978-1-62832-304-7 (pbk)
ISBN 978-1-56660-744-5 (eBook)
1. Rays (Fishes)—Juvenile literature. I. Title. II. Series: Living wild.

QL638.8.G57 2016
597.3/5—dc23   2015026825

CCSS: RI.5.1, 2, 3, 8; RST.6-8.1, 2, 5, 6, 8; RH.6-8.3, 4, 5, 6, 7, 8

First Edition HC 9 8 7 6 5 4 3 2 1
First Edition PBK 9 8 7 6 5 4 3 2 1

CREATIVE EDUCATION • CREATIVE PAPERBACKS

RAYS

Melissa Gish

In the shallow waters along Guam's
southern coast, a bluespotted stingray

glides effortlessly among corals and sponges.

In the shallow waters along Guam's southern coast, a bluespotted stingray glides effortlessly among corals and sponges. The 17-inch-wide (43.2 cm) female curls her wings and tilts her body to maneuver through the reef. She is headed toward the mangrove forest along the shores of Apra Harbor. Among the tangled mangrove roots, the ray finds a secluded spot to settle down. Her olive green coloration helps her blend into the muddy seabed. Her

underbelly is swollen. She has been carrying seven offspring, called pups, since early October. Now the time has come for the ray to give birth. One by one, the pups emerge, tail first. Their bodies are rolled up like slimy little burritos. The pups unfurl their wings and immediately dart for cover, disappearing into the murky shadows. Within minutes, the pups are left on their own as the mother ray swims back to the reef.

WHERE IN THE WORLD THEY LIVE

■ **Longtail Butterfly Ray**
Red Sea and coastlines of Indian Ocean throughout Southeast Asia

■ **Reef Manta Ray**
tropical and subtropical Indian and Pacific oceans; Red Sea

■ **Red Stingray**
Southeast Asian coastlines from Japan to Malaysia

■ **Caribbean Electric Ray**
Gulf of Mexico and Caribbean Sea

■ **Bullseye Electric Ray**
eastern Pacific coastlines from Mexico to Ecuador

More than 160 ray species inhabit Earth's tropical and subtropical waters. Many ray species prefer shallow coastlines, but some traverse deep ocean waters. Fewer in number, freshwater rays live in warm rivers and lakes. The colored squares represent the areas in which five ray species are found today.

FLAT-OUT WEIRD

Rays are some of the largest and most diverse fish on the planet. They inhabit Earth's tropical seas, from shallow reefs to deep **trenches**. Because their skeletons are made of firm, flexible body tissue called cartilage instead of bone, they are members of the class Chondrichthyes (*kon-DRIK-thee-ees*), as are their shark relatives. About 200 million years ago, some shark species began to change, **evolving** into rays. Rays have flat bodies and wide fins—a shape shared by the more than 450 fish in the superorder Batoidea. Batoids also include skates and sawfish. The more than 160 species of ray comprise 10 families in the order Myliobatiformes. This name is derived from the Greek words *mylio*, meaning "mill" (which refers to the ray's grinding teeth), and *bathos*, meaning "deep" (which refers to the ocean).

Some rays, such as spotted eagle rays, live exclusively along shallow coastlines, while others roam the deep sea. Some rays are freshwater fish. The pincushion ray inhabits lakes and rivers in West Africa. The roughback whipray, one of the smallest rays, can be found only in two rivers in western Thailand. In Florida, the abundant Atlantic

The only two known specimens of giant stumptail stingray were found in Russia's Peter the Great Bay.

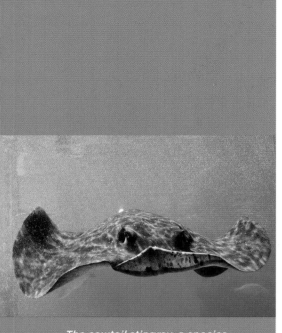

The cowtail stingray, a species fished for its skin (to produce a leather called shagreen), moves by undulation.

Like sharks, rays have skin with denticles, which are small toothlike projections that all point in the same direction, like scales.

stingray inhabits the St. Johns River and many inland freshwater lakes.

As batoids, rays' eyes are positioned on the top of the body, while the mouth, nostrils, and gill slits are on the bottom. A whiplike tail helps distinguish rays from other batoids. Like all fish, rays breathe through gills. As rays swim, water is forced over the gills, where thin layers of tissue collect oxygen and transfer it into the ray's bloodstream. While resting on the ocean floor, rays breathe by using spiracles (small slits behind each eye) to pump water over their gills. All rays have five pairs of gills except for one species, the sixgill stingray, a deepwater inhabitant of the Indian and Pacific oceans.

Rays have several types of fins used for **propulsion**, steering, and balance. The two pectoral fins that extend outward from the sides of the body are called wings. (The body is called the disc.) Wings help rays move through the water. Some ray species flutter the edges of their wings in a motion called undulation, while other species flap their wings up and down like the wings of a bird— oscillation. One or two pairs of pelvic fins on the lower body keep the ray from rolling over as it swims forward.

The southern Atlantic stingray swims by oscillation, causing it to look like a bird flying through the water.

Thorntail stingrays can grow to nearly six feet (1.8 m) in width and weigh up to 440 pounds (200 kg).

These fins may be distinctly visible as curved limbs, or they may be indistinguishable from the rest of the disc. Unlike their shark relatives, which use back and tail fins for balance and propulsion, rays have only a slender, muscular tail used for steering.

Ray species known as stingrays have one or two spines near the base of the tail. These sharp spines, called barbs, are serrated and look like double-edged steak knives. They secrete poisonous venom that affects the heart and respiratory system of living creatures that are stabbed by the barbs. Some barbs are visible, while others are concealed within a sheath and emerge only when the stingray strikes. Barbs are the stingray's only form of defense. When threatened, stingrays will choose first to swim away. If escape is impossible, a stingray will lift its tail and release its barb with lightning speed into the flesh of its victim. The entire barb may stick in a wound, or the tip may break off. The stingray regrows its barb at a rate of about one-half to three-quarters of an inch (1.3–1.9 cm) per month.

Stingray venom is powerful enough to kill other sea creatures, but it is rarely fatal in humans. About 22 species

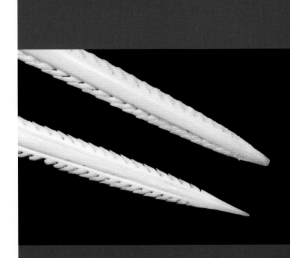

Though stingray barbs are sharp, they are made of cartilage, the same flexible material featured in a ray's skeleton.

Electric rays have organs capable of producing 14 to 37 volts of electricity, which they use in defense and to stun prey.

of stingray frequent the coastal waters of the United States, causing roughly 2,000 injuries to humans every year. Most injuries occur because people inadvertently step on stingrays while wading or unintentionally catch stingrays on fishing lines and then mishandle them. Barbs are sharp enough to cut through veins, arteries, and other body parts, and if not removed immediately, they can cause serious infections.

Rays vary in color from brown to gray to black, and many have markings that help them blend in with the ocean floor when resting and feeding. They are typically dark on top and light on the bottom. This type of **camouflage** is called countershading. When light strikes the ray from above, it creates a shadow on the fish's lighter underside and makes it less detectable from below. This helps rays to avoid predators while swimming. Rays vary greatly in size, from the 24-inch-wide (61 cm) Atlantic stingray to the 8-foot-wide (2.4 m) spiny butterfly ray to the 22-foot-wide (6.7 m) giant manta—the largest ray in the world, weighing up to 3,000 pounds (1,361 kg).

Unlike skates, which actively hunt fish, rays eat small fish only if an easy opportunity presents itself. Some rays

Camouflaging itself against the seafloor is a ray's strongest form of defense against sharks and other predators.

The markings on a manta ray's underbelly are like fingerprints—no two individuals share the same pattern.

eat mostly mollusks, shellfish, and other crustaceans, which they crush and grind with their powerful teeth. Other rays swallow massive amounts of tiny krill and **plankton**. Tiny pores that look like dark spots around the mouth are called the ampullae of Lorenzini. Pores that run from the snout to the tail are lateral line organs. These two special sensory systems help rays locate prey. The organs detect differences in energy signals, such as vibrations made by prey moving along or under the ocean floor.

Ray teeth are arranged in rows along the top and bottom jaws. Some rays have 30 to 40 rows, while others, such as the giant manta, have 300 rows. The size of each tooth varies by species as well. A giant manta's teeth are each the size of a pinhead, but other ray teeth are larger. The rows are arranged in a pattern called quincunx (like the five spots on dice) to form a solid grinding surface. Every one to two weeks, as teeth are broken or worn down, replacement teeth move forward. Some rays may go through hundreds of thousands of teeth in a lifetime. Ray teeth are shiny because, like human teeth, they contain the mineral compound calcium hydroxyapatite— the main component of tooth enamel.

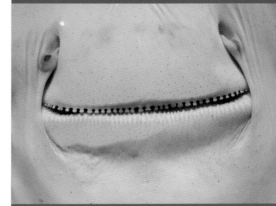

A ray's teeth are connected to its jaws by structures called upper and lower tooth bands.

Manta and devil rays are fished for their black gill rakers, which are commonly used in traditional Southeast Asian medicines.

FLYING AND FLOPPING

Rays do not have ripping teeth, so they can eat only prey small enough to fit in their mouths. Rays either swallow their food whole or crush it with their rows of flat teeth. Most rays typically remain in areas where food is abundant, such as coral reefs and **estuaries**, but some ray species will circle Earth's oceans to follow **migrating** prey. Traveling rays include the two species of manta and nine species of devil ray. These are the only rays that have evolved into filter feeders. They swim with their mouths open, taking in water with the help of two curved fins, called lobes, on their head. As water passes through the gills, tiny projections called gill rakers capture food.

Seasonal changes trigger an instinct in some ray species to gather in massive schools to feed. Around the islands of the Maldives, shifting currents in the Indian Ocean during the summer **monsoon** season (May to November) drive large numbers of krill and plankton to shallow waters. Reef mantas, which normally prefer to be alone, gather by the hundreds to feed on the bounty. These rays average 12 feet (3.7 m) from wingtip to wingtip. As many

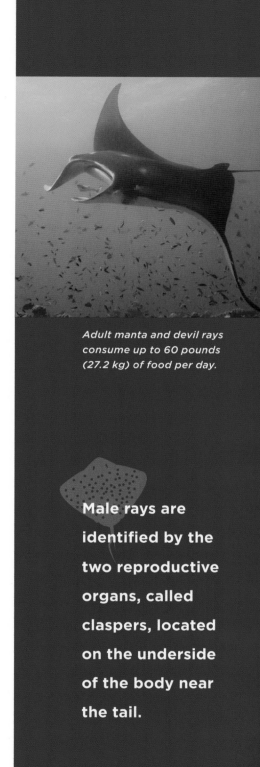

Adult manta and devil rays consume up to 60 pounds (27.2 kg) of food per day.

Male rays are identified by the two reproductive organs, called claspers, located on the underside of the body near the tail.

Small, young manta rays often swim in schools as a measure of protection from predators such as sharks.

as 200 of them may gracefully maneuver around each other, gulping down tiny, **nutrient**-rich organisms in areas no bigger than a football field.

Other rays ambush their food. Masters of camouflage, the rays lie on the seabed, sometimes partially buried, for long periods of time, waiting to nab shrimp, snails, or other prey. Two new species of these ambush predators were discovered in the Amazon River in 2011 by researchers at the University of São Paulo. Commonly called pancake rays, the two rays in the genus *Heliotrygon* are very flat and almost perfectly circular in shape. Their coloration makes them easily blend in with the river's muddy bottom. When unsuspecting fish or freshwater shrimp come along, the rays lift their bodies, snatch their prey, and return to their hiding position—all in the blink of an eye.

Still other rays swim through shallow coastal habitats, casually patrolling for food. Cownose rays, which are common in the bays of New England, locate clams, oysters, and scallops in beds of seagrass. Using their mouths like a vacuum, the rays pull these creatures free of their anchors. Spotted eagle rays flap their fins over the floors of reef habitats to stir up sand, exposing buried mollusks and marine worms. It seems as though the quest for food never stops for rays. Researchers are still trying to determine whether rays truly sleep, as studies have shown them to appear ever watchful for prey, even when motionless for long periods of time on the seafloor. And like most of their shark relatives, mantas and devil rays must keep moving at all times to survive.

After feeding, the second strongest instinct in rays is reproducing. Rays are often confused with skates, but reproduction is one way of telling the two animals apart:

Bluntnose stingrays spend summers in bays and estuaries of the U.S. Atlantic coast before going south in winter.

Skate egg cases are made of collagen, a fine but tough fiber found only in the tissues and eggs of animals.

Rays can practice embryonic diapause, keeping fertilized eggs as tiny balls of cells until conditions are just right.

Skates are oviparous (*oh-VIP-uh-rus*), meaning they lay eggs. Rays are ovoviviparous (*OH-voh-vy-VIP-uh-rus*), meaning their young develop in eggs and hatch while still inside the mother. The babies continue to grow until they leave her body, fully formed. However, little else is known about ray reproduction. Of the more than 450 batoids, scientists have observed only 5 species mating in the wild.

Smaller rays, which have short life cycles, become sexually mature between ages two and four. However, larger rays—such as devil rays—are not ready to mate until they are 10, and mantas must be 15 to 20. Rays gather in groups to select mates. Courtship involves swimming close together while males nip at females' fins. After mating, the males leave the females to carry their young for 60 days to 12 months, depending on the species.

The yolk within the egg feeds the embryo (unhatched offspring) for the initial stages of development. Then the growing embryo ingests or absorbs a nutrient-rich milk substance (called histotroph) that the mother produces and secretes into her **uterus**. The pups grow until they are strong enough to leave their mother's body. The number of pups born can be as many as 15 every year or,

Some ray species migrate to specific breeding grounds before they begin their courtship behaviors.

Bony fish can quickly rise and drop like a helicopter, but sharks and rays move smoothly like an airplane.

in the case of the giant manta, as few as 1 pup every 2 to 3 years. Newborn pups are left completely on their own.

Sharks pose the greatest natural threat to rays, so juvenile rays tend to stay in shallow coastal waters, near coral reefs, or buried in the seabed until they grow large and fast enough to avoid being eaten. Reef and coastal rays are most active during the day, when they can see predators approaching. After dark, these rays settle to the ocean floor to hide from the sharks that become more active at night. Reef mantas simply disappear at dusk.

Researchers have tried to figure out where they go, but the nighttime rituals of these rays remain a mystery.

The life span of rays is related to their size, with most species living between 8 and 15 years. Giant mantas are believed to live as long as 40 years. Throughout their lives, rays make regular visits to particular reefs around the world known as cleaning stations. Rays and other large predatory fish have a special relationship with small reef fish. The reef fish nibble the bigger fish's skin, eating **parasites** such as sea lice as well as damaged tissue, which speeds healing of wounds. Rays often even allow cleaner fish to safely enter their mouths to remove bits of food from their teeth.

Another way that rays keep their skin clean is by swimming at high speeds and then leaping out of the water. The bellyflop landing sends parasites flying off. In 2008, a Florida boater was killed when an 8-foot-wide (2.4 m) spotted eagle ray leaped from the water and accidentally hit her. In 2012, National Geographic filmmakers captured rare footage of tens of thousands of 12-foot-wide (3.7 m) devil rays leaping and bellyflopping in the waters off Mexico's Baja California for several hours before disappearing into the ocean depths.

Leopoldi, or black diamond, stingrays are freshwater rays found only in the rivers of Brazil.

A 15-foot (4.6 m) ray can swim about 9 miles (14.5 km) per hour; larger rays can swim up to 22 miles (35.4 km) per hour.

Rays and other fish were popular subjects in the Japanese art form of ukiyo-e, using woodblock prints.

Sea creatures are common symbols in the **cultural** history of many native peoples of the Americas, including the ancient peoples of Mesoamerica, an area from Mexico into Central America. These people included sharks and rays in their traditions and **mythology**. Pottery featuring rays found in southern Panama dates back to more than 1,000 years ago. The rays were shaped from clay, painted with spots, and then attached to plates and vases. The carvings likely represent spotted eagle rays or round stingrays, both common in Panama's coastal waters.

Archaeologists believe that the Mesoamericans included the relationship between stingrays and sharks as part of their cultural symbolism. Large sharks prey upon stingrays, and shark jaws embedded with stingray barbs have been found at burial sites in Panama. These were likely symbols of the natural order of life and death, which was important to the Mesoamericans.

Because stingray barbs are razor-sharp, the Mesoamericans used them in a ritual called bloodletting, in which a person was pierced with a sharp object and

Featuring a spotted stingray and other fish, this Greek plate from about 350 B.C. was used in funeral rituals.

The South American freshwater ocellate river stingray is a ray species commonly kept in zoos and aquariums.

Ocellate river stingrays are also called peacock-eye stingrays because their ringed spots resemble those on peacock tail feathers.

made to bleed. The rituals were public events, with people gathering around the base of a mound or pyramid to watch. The idea was to show gratitude to the gods by giving back some part of the body that the gods had given to humans. Stingray barbs were some of the most commonly used tools in the rituals. Sometimes the skin was only poked, but other times a slender rope was tied to the end of a stingray barb that was then pulled completely through the tongue, earlobe, or other body part. Such rituals continued until the 1600s.

People the world over learned just how lethal stingray barbs can be when they heard the tragic news of the death of Steve Irwin, better known as "The Crocodile Hunter." On September 4, 2006, Irwin and his cameraman were filming an 8-foot-wide (2.4 m) bull stingray in the Great Barrier Reef. The fish, likely mistaking Irwin for a tiger shark (its greatest predator), stabbed Irwin numerous times in the chest before fleeing. The stingray's barb, the size of a steak knife, pierced Irwin's heart and lung, killing him within minutes.

Despite many ray species possessing potentially dangerous barbs, rays are a popular attraction for snorkelers and divers today. Hundreds of southern stingrays have made

two particular dive spots in the Cayman Islands their permanent home because they are fed daily by humans who invite tourists to swim with them. Olowalu Reef in Hawaii is a well-known cleaning station that many scuba divers visit to see reef mantas and other shallow-water wildlife. Similar tourist attractions around the world allow people to swim with rays. However, some conservation biologists are afraid such human interaction may negatively influence rays' natural behaviors and affect the long-term health of these fish.

As strange creatures with unique characteristics, rays are typically depicted as dangerous characters in popular

Petting a ray's skin in one direction feels like Jell-O®, but stroking the other direction feels like sandpaper.

The suit worn by Marvel hero Stingray takes its winglike design from the pectoral fins of the animal.

culture. Black Manta, a supervillain in the DC Comics world, debuted in September 1967. **Genetically** engineered to breathe underwater, and wearing a black wetsuit with a helmet capable of shooting destructive beams from the eyes, he became the archenemy of Aquaman. Marvel Comics' Stingray debuted at the same time as Black Manta. Stingray wears a super-strong, artificial-cartilage suit designed to withstand the crushing pressure of deep-sea diving and recycle oxygen for unlimited underwater breathing. Borrowing from the traits of the electric ray, Stingray can shoot 20,000 volts of electricity through his gloves. Rather than acting as a villain, however, Stingray often aids Captain America, Iron Man, and the other Avengers in fighting the forces of evil.

Depth Charge is a ray character in the Transformers world. Pulled through a glitch in space-time and exposed to strange radiation, his manta body was "Transmetalized," giving him the power to fight in the Beast Wars. An entire culture of manta-like creatures is the focus of Timothy Zahn's 2002 science-fiction book, *Manta's Gift*. When a young man is injured in a skiing accident, he agrees to have his brain transplanted into the body of a Qanska, one

Black Manta was a treasure hunter and mercenary before hatred for Aquaman caused him to become a supervillain.

In 1942, the USS Stingray gained two forward torpedo tubes to increase the submarine's firing power in World War II.

of the manta-like aliens with superior technology that fly through the atmosphere of Jupiter. The literary classic *The Black Pearl* (1967) by Scott O'Dell depicts a very different relationship between humans and rays. In the book, a giant manta named Manta Diablo guards a priceless black pearl and has killed many people from a small fishing village. Ramon Salazar, a courageous boy from the village, vows to defeat the manta.

The fierce appearance of giant rays has inspired sports teams to adopt their likenesses. The Tampa Bay Rays is a Major League Baseball team that began play in 1998 as the Tampa Bay Devil Rays and shortened its name 10 years later. Though the team mascot is Raymond, a furry blue creature called a seadog, the team's logo is a giant manta. A navy blue and red stingray is the logo of the South Carolina Stingrays, a team in the East Coast Hockey League. Less intimidating than the team logo is the Stingrays' mascot, Cool Ray, who has his own Facebook page.

Stingrays have inspired the design and naming of vehicles as well. The USS *Stingray* became one of the most famous submarines in U.S. history. Launched in 1937 and sent into battle 16 times during World War II, the *Stingray*

holds the record for the most war patrols of any U.S. submarine. As a wartime vessel, the *Stingray* lived up to its animal namesake's reputation for delivering quick, deadly blows to its enemies. Perhaps the best-known mechanical ray is the Corvette Stingray. Introduced in 1963, it cost about $3,500 and was made famous by the Beach Boys and other musicians as well as movie stars such as Elvis Presley and James Dean. Today's Stingray, starting at more than 15 times the cost of the original model, has maintained a reputation as one of America's most admired sports cars. As a symbol of American pride, it was even featured prominently in the 2014 Marvel Studios movie *Captain America: The Winter Soldier.*

Car designer Bill Mitchell was inspired by a deep-sea fishing experience to create the Corvette Stingray.

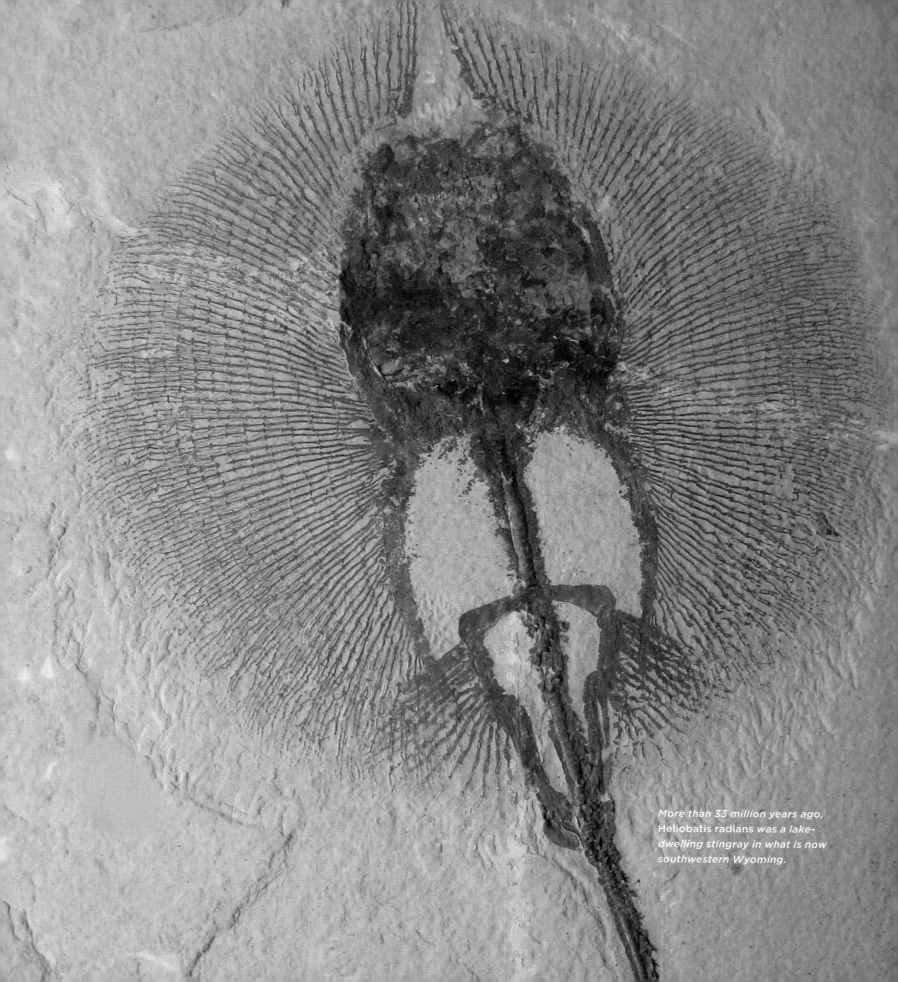

More than 33 million years ago, *Heliobatis radians* was a lake-dwelling stingray in what is now southwestern Wyoming.

Very little is known about ray evolution because, as cartilaginous fish, they left few traces in the fossil record. Rays are as old as the first dinosaurs, yet they have remained mostly unchanged from their ancestors. Despite 200 million years of evolution, rays are in serious trouble. Nearly one-third of ray species are labeled as vulnerable, endangered, or critically endangered on the Red List of Threatened Species that is published annually by the International Union for Conservation of Nature (IUCN). Many more species are believed to be in trouble, but they do not appear on the IUCN list because not enough research has been collected to classify their status.

As advancements in technology allow us to probe ever deeper into the oceans, researchers are able to better understand some of Earth's most elusive marine life. One person who has dedicated her life to mantas is Dr. Andrea Marshall, an American conservation biologist living in Mozambique. When Marshall completed her PhD in the study of mantas in 2008, she became the first person in the world to earn such a degree. Her commitment to

An Australian stamp featured a stingaree, the eastern shore's most abundant shallow-water ray.

The New Ireland stingaree, named for the site of its discovery in the Bismarck Archipelago, has thorny projections on its back.

Mantas favor waters warmer than 70 °F (21.1 °C), but extra blood vessels in the brain help them function in colder water.

mantas led to the formation of the Marine Megafauna Foundation, an organization that focuses on the research and conservation of large animals such as rays, sharks, marine **mammals**, and sea turtles. Wishing to educate the public about the plight of mantas, Marshall became the subject of a 2009 BBC documentary, *Andrea Marshall: Queen of Mantas*.

Marshall's research team is based at southern Mozambique's Tofo Beach, the site of a major cleaning station for mantas. Until Marshall began studying mantas, very little was known about these creatures' lives. But after hundreds of dives to swim with the mantas, Marshall made several important discoveries. What was once thought to be a single manta species is actually two separate species with varying biology, habitat use, and social behavior. Also, mantas are far more intelligent than previously thought. Marshall says of mantas, "They are incredibly majestic and gentle creatures, but they have a distinct curiosity that is absent in so many of the other sharks and rays." For instance, instead of swimming away from divers, mantas seek to interact with them.

To study mantas, Marshall attached **satellite**-tracking devices to the mantas' bodies. The data revealed valuable information about the rays' migrations and habits. They travel long distances in short periods of time, and they regularly dive to depths of more than 4,500 feet (1,372 m). Photography is a valuable tool in Marshall's research as well. Each manta has a unique set of dark markings on its white underbelly. To identify the 650 individual mantas frequenting Tofo, Marshall photographed the mantas' markings and named each ray after the image she saw in

Manta rays take their name from the Spanish word manta, *which means "cloak" or "blanket."*

The spotted eagle ray's tail can be up to three times longer than the width of the ray's body.

their markings. To share her own findings and collect information from others, Marshall created MantaMatcher .org, a website where the public can contribute photographs of mantas' underbellies to a global database.

Over a span of just 10 years, Marshall's research revealed an 88 percent decline in the manta population in her Mozambique study site. This was mainly caused by overfishing for the mantas' gill rakers, which are used in some traditional Chinese remedies. Armed with this data, Marshall successfully rallied to get mantas added to three major conservation lists: the IUCN Red List; the Convention on Migratory Species (CMS), an international organization dedicated to species conservation; and the Convention on International Trade in Endangered Species of Wild Fauna and Flora (CITES), which regulates the global trade of animals and animal products.

Another ray species that is finally getting much-needed scientific attention is the spotted eagle ray. Although a protected species in the U.S., this ray is vulnerable to fishing for its meat in nearby waters, especially in Mexico and Cuba. In 2009, Florida's Mote Marine Laboratory & Aquarium launched a project to study the distribution, migration, feeding habits, reproduction, and growth rates of this ray. The IUCN lists the spotted eagle ray as near-threatened with a decreasing population trend.

Biologists at Mote Marine Laboratory have studied hundreds of spotted eagle rays off the southwestern Florida coast. The scientists measure the rays and collect blood samples for genetic analysis. Then they attach identification tags to the animals before releasing them. So far, the research has led to a better understanding

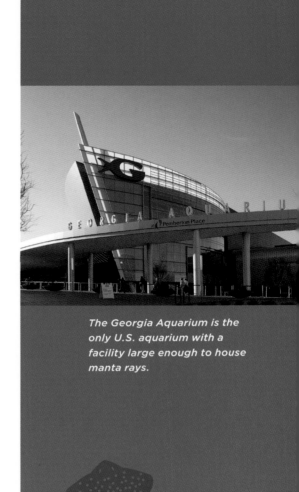

The Georgia Aquarium is the only U.S. aquarium with a facility large enough to house manta rays.

Atlanta's Georgia Aquarium is home to Nandi, a manta accidentally caught in shark nets off South Africa in 2007.

The spotted pattern of the marbled whipray's disc helps it blend in with its rocky seabed habitat.

of the rays' population structure and migratory habits in the Gulf of Mexico. As the rays swim close to the water's surface, they can be observed by airplane and boat. Such surveys by Mote Marine Laboratory researchers have revealed declining numbers as fishing pressure ramps up. The researchers hope to increase awareness of the spotted eagle ray's plight and reduce the demand for this ray species.

Research being conducted in Thailand is geared at saving not only rays but also humans. Bangkok's Chulalongkorn University joined forces with Fishsiam (*FISH-sy-AM*), a recreational fishing guide service, to capture and study giant freshwater stingrays. Growing up to 16 feet (4.9 m) wide, these are the world's largest river fish. Fishsiam guides catch the stingrays in the Ban Pakong and other Thai rivers. Then veterinarians take blood samples and measurements and attach identification tags to the rays. The stingrays' venom, which can be deadly to humans, is collected, in hopes of developing **antivenom** for it. Giant freshwater stingrays naturally avoid humans, but since this fish's discovery in 1990, sport fishermen have hunted it. This sometimes leads

to deadly encounters with the rays' 15-inch (38.1 cm) barb—a weapon powerful enough to penetrate bone.

In addition to the effects of global **climate change**, habitat destruction, and ocean pollution, the number-one cause of ray species' decline is overfishing. Because so little research is conducted on rays, few conservation strategies exist. Global efforts for funding and research will be required to protect and more fully understand these mysterious, charismatic creatures.

In Brazil, the spotted eagle ray's nickname (pintada) *is after the guinea fowl, a spotted bird the ray resembles.*

ANIMAL TALE: GREAT MANTA CHASES THE SUN

Animals of the sky and sea have been part of the cultural and religious traditions of Hinduism for thousands of years, since the earliest gods and goddesses were described in the Vedas, the oldest holy writings in the Hindu religion. The following myth featuring Varuna, the god of the ocean, and Usha, the daughter of the sky, tells how the manta came to inhabit the Arabian Sea.

Every morning, Usha spread her arms and lifted the sun into the sky. The birds awakened and sang joyful songs as they flew all over the land. One particular bird, Little Myna, had great curiosity. She would chase the sun, wanting to learn its secrets. Try as she might, though, Little Myna could never reach the sun.

"Little Myna," laughed the other myna birds, "you are foolish. You will never catch the sun!"

Little Myna would not give up, so one day she followed the sun all the way to the seashore. In the evening, as Usha began to fold her arms and lower the sun, Little Myna watched the seabirds fly out to sea. She decided to follow them.

Little Myna's wings were small, and she quickly tired. As the sun disappeared below the horizon, Little Myna realized that she was far from shore. She called out, "Varuna, please help me!"

Varuna sent a sea turtle to Little Myna. "You do not belong at sea," Varuna scolded as Little Myna settled onto the sea turtle's back. "Perhaps I should turn you into a turtle."

"No, no," said Little Myna. "I love to fly. Please do not take away my wings." Then the sea turtle carried Little Myna back to shore.

The next evening, Little Myna thought for sure she could reach the sun, so she followed the seabirds. She tired before her journey was half over. In the dim light, she cried out, "Please help me, Varuna!"

This time, Varuna sent a great whale, who opened its mouth and let Little Myna settle on its tongue. "You are not made for the sea," Varuna told Little Myna. "I should turn you into a whale."

"No, no," Little Myna pleaded. "I love my wings." Then the whale carried Little Myna back to shore.

Still curious to learn the sun's secrets, Little Myna once again went to the seashore and flew toward the sun. And once again, she weakened long before reaching it. "Varuna, please help me!" she called.

Varuna had no more patience for Little Myna and sent no one to help her. Unable to flap her wings any longer, Little Myna fell into the sea. She tried to swim, flailing her wings and kicking her spindly legs, but she could not stay above the water. She slipped beneath the waves, certain she would drown.

Varuna took pity on Little Myna. Suddenly, the bird's legs transformed into a long, slender tail, and her wings stretched into broad fins. Her beak curled into lobes, and her eyes grew huge. Instead of drowning, she felt herself gliding. She was flying underwater! No longer was she Little Myna. She had become Great Manta!

"You want to reach the sun," Varuna said to her. "Go chase it!" And that is what the manta does to this day.

GLOSSARY

antivenom – a substance created to counteract the effects of a venom

archaeologists – people who study human history by examining ancient peoples and their artifacts

camouflage – the ability to hide, due to coloring or markings that blend in with a given environment

climate change – the gradual increase in Earth's temperature that causes changes in the planet's atmosphere, environments, and long-term weather conditions

cultural – of or relating to particular groups in a society that share behaviors and characteristics that are accepted as normal by that group

estuaries – the mouths of large rivers, where the tides (from oceans or seas) meet the streams

evolving – gradually developing into a new form

genetically – relating to genes, the basic physical units of heredity

mammals – warm-blooded animals that have a backbone and hair or fur, give birth to live young, and produce milk to feed their young

migrating – undertaking a seasonal journey from one place to another and then back again

monsoon – the seasonal wind that brings rain in Southeast Asia and India

mythology – a collection of myths, or popular, traditional beliefs or stories that explain how something came to be or that are associated with a person or object

nutrient – a substance that gives an animal energy and helps it grow

parasites – animals or plants that live on or inside another living thing (called a host) while giving nothing back to the host; some parasites cause disease or even death

plankton – algae and animals that drift or float in the ocean, many of which are microscopic

propulsion – forward movement created by using energy

satellite – a mechanical device launched into space; it may be designed to travel around Earth or toward other planets or the sun

trenches – long, narrow, steep-sided ditches in the earth's crust

uterus – the organ in a female animal's body where offspring develop before birth; another word for "womb"

SELECTED BIBLIOGRAPHY

Kells, Val, and Kent Carpenter. *A Field Guide to Coastal Fishes: From Maine to Texas*. Baltimore: Johns Hopkins University Press, 2011.

Klimely, A. Peter. *The Biology of Sharks and Rays*. Chicago: University of Chicago Press, 2013.

Marine Megafauna Foundation. "Queen of Mantas." http://www.queenofmantas.com.

National Geographic. "Photo Gallery: Rays." http://ocean.nationalgeographic.com/ocean/photos/ocean-rays.

Ross, Richard. *Freshwater Stingrays: Everything about Purchase, Care, Feeding, and Aquarium Design*. Hauppauge, N.Y.: Barron's, 1999.

Siddall, Mark. *Poison: Sinister Species with Deadly Consequences*. New York: Sterling, 2014.

Note: Every effort has been made to ensure that any websites listed above were active at the time of publication. However, because of the nature of the Internet, it is impossible to guarantee that these sites will remain active indefinitely or that their contents will not be altered.

Rays are timid creatures that help maintain the balance of the ocean's fragile environment.

INDEX